Medicine
Now

Anne Rooney

Chrysalis Education

Artificial Intelligence
Genetic Engineering
Internet Technologies
Medicine Now

Distributed in the United States by

Smart Apple Media, 1980 Lookout Drive, North Mankato, Minnesota 56003

Copyright © Chrysalis Books PLC 2003

ISBN 1-59389-121-0

The Library of Congress control number 2003104919

Editorial manager	Joyce Bentley
Editor:	Susie Brooks
Designer:	John Jamieson
Consultant:	Helen Cameron
Picture researcher:	Louise Daubeny

Also thanks to: Gill Adams, Pip Hardy and Penny Worms

Anne Rooney asserts her moral right to be recognized as the author of this work.
If you have any comments on this book, please email her at anne@annerooney.co.uk.
For more information on her work, visit www.annerooney.co.uk.

Printed in Hong Kong

Picture Acknowledgements
All reasonable efforts have been made to trace the relevant copyright holders of the images contained within this
book. If we were unable to reach you, please contact Chrysalis Children's Books.
B = bottom; L = left; R = right; T = top
Cover © Royalty-Free/CORBIS 1 Dr Yorgos Nikas/Science Photo Library 4 Mary Evans Picture Library 5 © Royalty-
Free/CORBIS 6 © H. Davies/Exile Images 7 T Getty Images 7 B Prof. P. Motta/Dept. of Anatomy/University, 'La Sapienza',
Rome/Science Photo Library 8 Jim James/PA Photos 9 T Kirsty Wigglesworth/PA Photos 9 B Geoff du Feu/RSPCA
Photolibrary 10 © Alison Wright/CORBIS 11 SUYK/Rex Features 12 Image State 13 © Jose Luis Pelaez, Inc./CORBIS 14/15
B © Patrick Bennett/CORBIS 15 R Klaus Guldbrandsen/Science Photo Library 16 Klaus Guldbrandsen/Science Photo Library
17 T © Stephanie Maze/CORBIS 17 B © Joseph Sohm; ChromoSohm Inc./CORBIS 18 Joseph Nettis/Science Photo Library
19 Rex Features 20 Hank Morgan/Science Photo Library 21 © Dennis Galante/CORBIS 22 © David Pollack/CORBIS 23 ©
Ariel Skelley/CORBIS 24 D. Ell, Publiphoto Diffusion/Science Photo Library 25 © ER Productions/CORBIS 26 PA Photos/
European Press Agency 27 T © Chuck Savage/CORBIS 27 B Getty Images 28 Alex Bartel/Science Photo Library 29
Alexander Tsiaras/Science Photo Library 30 © H.Davies/Exile Images 31 T © Dale O'Dell/CORBIS 31 B Jim Arbogast/
Photodisc 32 © Bettmann/CORBIS 33 © RSPCA Photolibrary 34 Getty Images 35 Mary Evans Picture Library 36 Dr Yorgos
Nikas/Science Photo Library 37 J.L. Martra, Publiphoto Diffusion/Science Photo Library 38 © Andrew Forsyth/ RSPCA
Photolibrary 39 Getty Images 40 Carlos Goldin/Science Photo Library 41 T © Keren Su/CORBIS 41 B reproduced by kind
permission of Tesco 42 Getty Images 43 The Advertising Archive Ltd. 44 © Advocates for Animals/ACIG/RSPCA
Photolibrary 45 CC Studio/Science Photo Library.

Contents

Modern medicine

When we are ill or injured, we expect those caring for us to do all they can to make us better. As medical science changes, treatments become more varied, more advanced, and more effective. But can modern medicine present problems, too?

New ways of treating disease are often complicated and expensive. They may have been developed in ways that people regard as wrong, or unethical. Sometimes patients don't want treatment they're given—or they'd prefer no treatment at all. How much say should we have in what we allow medical professionals to do?

Definition: ethics

Ethics is the study of what is right and wrong. Some people believe there is an absolute code of ethics—things "are" right or wrong—others think that we make up our own ethical codes, which may be different in different societies.

In this book we'll look at how the ways we treat the sick are changing, and think about some of the questions these changes raise. There may be no "right" answers, but they are intriguing issues that we must all think about if we're to have a say in how our world develops.

This book won't tell you what to think. It will give you some scientific background and present many different views and possibilities. Then you can think about and discuss the issues, forming your own opinions—opinions that you are able to explain and defend.

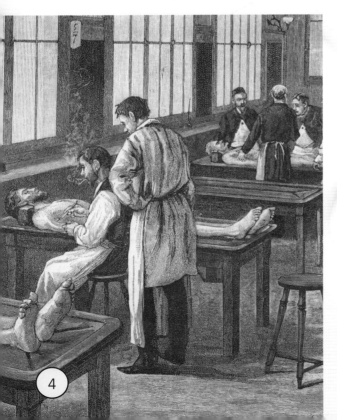

In the 19th century, medical research was often carried out on the corpses of people who couldn't afford a burial. Many people feared that this would prevent their souls going to heaven. Should doctors have been allowed to cut up bodies without the relatives' permission?

Medicine's frontiers

Medical researchers are trying all the time to find new ways to treat illness, care for patients, and help people to have long and healthy lives. We can now cure diseases, lessen pain, and use tiny pieces of machinery or body parts from people who've died to replace unhealthy limbs or organs. We can even keep seriously ill people alive against all odds. But should we really be prolonging life at any cost?

Modern medicine is a complex science—it doesn't just involve doctors and nurses. Researchers and lab technicians also play a vital part, carrying out tests and developing new drugs.

Progress in research

Medical discoveries are the products of hard work. Scientists spend a lot of time and money exploring disease and developing new treatments. Some research involves the use of material from dead bodies, or from animals, or from very early human embryos that have not been allowed to grow into babies. The treatments developed are tested for a long time on animals and on humans. Some people object to these processes— how can we decide what's acceptable?

Medicine and money

Most new treatments and pieces of medical equipment are developed by commercial businesses. These companies need to make money from their work or they won't be able to fund new research. But many medical companies are very rich—does this mean they're charging too much? What can we do to make expensive treatments available to people who can't afford them—to people in poorer countries, for example?

Modern medicine
The health industry

Medicine is big business. Some governments spend a lot of money on healthcare for the people in their countries. Others can't afford this, or just operate different systems.

Where you live matters

In the U.K. people who earn more than a minimum wage pay for the National Health Service (NHS) through taxes. The NHS aims to give people most of the treatment they need for free. Because of the demands on this type of healthcare, some people also buy private health insurance. This means that they pay an insurance company to cover the costs if they want to be treated quickly or to stay in a more comfortable hospital.

In some countries, private health-care systems are widely used. In the U.S., for example, most people buy insurance that will pay for any treatments they need. Free hospitals are available for people who can't afford this, but they may be less comfortable and less well-equipped.

In many poorer countries, there is no free system and so no healthcare available to the poorest people. Even

In parts of Senegal, Africa, lack of food and drinking water leads to widespread ill health. The government can provide only one doctor to 400,000 people. Overseas charities offer some help, but everyone has to pay at least a little for their care.

expensive treatments. Even areas such as mental health are neglected because they are less in the public eye. Much research has to be funded by charities, because governments and medical companies won't pay.

in private hospitals, the treatments available often don't match those in developed countries.

Funding research

Medical treatments are expensive to develop. If companies think they'll make a profit from their research, they'll invest more money in it. This usually means looking for treatments for diseases that affect a lot of people, such as cancer. Medicines for common ailments such as headaches and colds are also money-spinners. Most of us will willingly buy these treatments just to make our lives more pleasant, so it's worthwhile for drug companies to develop them.

But there are areas in which research is severely lacking, simply because less money would be made from any treatments developed. Rare illnesses, for example, affect too few people for medical companies to benefit. Illnesses that mostly affect people in poor countries make little money because sufferers can't afford

Avoiding illness

Preventive care—working to avoid disease in the first place—doesn't make drug companies much money. But it's a useful investment for governments as, if it works, fewer people will need expensive treatments later. The problem is, it's difficult to get people to change their lifestyles to avoid possible dangers they may not understand. In this area, healthcare and education must work together.

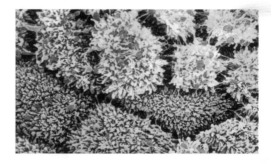

Free screening of the womb for cancer cells like these has meant fewer women get cervical cancer— but many women don't take up the offer of screening. Should it be made compulsory for all women?

7

Modern medicine
Beyond the frontiers

Governments play an important role in healthcare. As well as allocating money to medical services, and educating people to live healthy lives, they also have responsibility for other factors in society that affect our health. These can be anything from farming and food-processing methods to traffic control, pollution, and other environmental problems.

In 1990, U.K. government minister John Gummer encouraged the press to photograph his daughter eating a burger. He was trying to "prove" that British beef was safe from a fatal brain disease in cows, called BSE. Some people had developed a form of the disease and died.

Health risks

At the moment, people are worried that health problems may be caused by lead and other poisons in gasoline, crop pesticides, antibiotics fed to farm animals, genetically modified foods, cell phone transmitters, long-distance air travel, electricity towers—and many other things. Some factors we can control ourselves—we can choose not to smoke or use a cell phone too much—but others are beyond our control as individuals and we need our governments to act.

Electricity companies don't accept that living or spending a lot of time near electricity towers can damage people's health.

Other species

It's not only humankind we need to worry about. Some of the ways in which we are fighting disease affect other species, too. In recent years, smallpox has been wiped out around the world, and polio will soon follow. But bacteria and viruses such as these count as living species, so do we have the right to make them extinct?

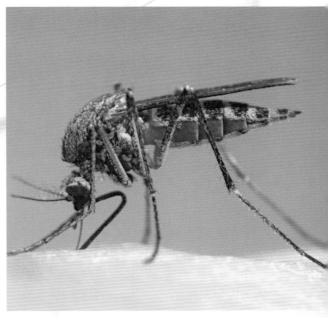

There are currently plans to replace normal mosquitoes with a genetically modified strain that can't carry malaria. This could save millions of lives—but are we entitled to change mosquitoes in the wild for our own ends?

Whose responsibility?

Often, it becomes obvious that something is a health risk only when people start to suffer. Medical issues then spill over into legal issues.

Some airplane passengers who have suffered blood clots believe that their problems were caused by sitting in cramped airplane seats for long periods of time. They have begun to sue the airlines for this. Some relatives of passengers who have died are trying to get compensation, too. Is it fair to blame the airlines, when a link between flying and blood clots has not been proven and has only become an issue quite recently?

What's it to you?

Why should you worry about modern medicine? If you're not ill and your family has no health problems, it may seem unimportant to you. But most of us need medical attention at some point in our lives, and it's in all of our interests to help protect the health of society as a whole. Healthcare is not just an issue when we're ill. How we live our lives affects our own health and that of others. We can all contribute to world healthcare. Here are a few general things to think about as you read the rest of this book.

Who counts?

In many areas of life we have to balance the needs of many different people. Medical care presents various problems of this type. Should we spend limited funds on prolonging the life of one person, or on easing suffering for many? Should we insist people have vaccinations to control disease fully, or should everyone be free to choose whether or not to be vaccinated? Does someone who has caused their own ill-health deserve the same free treatment as someone who couldn't help their condition?

Some people live in such appalling conditions that they have no chance of good health. Is this a local or international responsibility?

A global perspective

In many poorer countries, standards of health and healthcare are much lower than in richer countries. Millions of people die because of starvation, polluted water supplies, and diseases that could be cured or prevented. People suffer health problems as a result of war and natural disasters. Who should be responsible for healthcare in these poorer countries?

Some of the choices we make affect the well-being and health of people a long way away. Many people in poorer countries work in intolerable conditions making goods sold in richer countries, for instance. As global citizens, and as consumers who make choices about what we buy, we can make some difference.

Sweatshops in poorer countries cause ill health for many people. Should we provide healthcare for people who suffer making the things we buy?

Are there risks for us?

Many scientific developments may hold dangers of which we know nothing at the moment. Some types of medicine or treatment could have consequences we can't imagine. We have seen a few medical disasters in recent years—people catching AIDS from blood transfusions, for example, or new cures with horrible side effects. We can't be sure that some of the techniques we are trying now are entirely safe. Does the possibility of danger mean that some procedures or treatments shouldn't be tried? Who should decide?

Over to you

We all have a right to be involved in decisions about the world's future. But in order to have the power to change things, we need to understand the issues that affect us all. You will need to be able to separate fact from opinion in the things you read and hear. You will need to be able to disentangle reliable information from media scare stories and public relations hype. If you can do this, and shape your own informed views, you will be able to play an important part in the changing world. Use the "Ask yourself" boxes in the following chapters as a starting point for discussing the issues raised.

New life

One subject that people feel very strongly about in the area of healthcare is babies—how we treat people who can't easily have babies, how we cure sick babies, and what we do about unwanted pregnancies.

Fertility treatments

People who can't have a child of their own in the natural way will often try any treatment—even if it is difficult, unpleasant, or expensive—to help them conceive. Many use fertility drugs—medicines to boost their supply of sperm or eggs, or to increase their chances of an egg developing successfully in the womb.

Treatment may also involve taking an egg from the woman, or from another woman (an egg donor), and fertilizing it outside the body. This means combining it with sperm, either from the woman's partner or from another man (a sperm donor). A fertilized egg—which now has the potential to develop into a baby—is put back into her womb to grow and be born normally. This process is called in vitro fertilization, or IVF.

IVF may be used if either the man or the woman has a fertility problem —if they can't produce sperm or eggs properly, for example. Or it may be used if one or both partners has a dangerous inherited disease. In this case, sperm or egg donors who don't have the disease can be used. Or the couple may use their own eggs and sperm but have the embryos tested and only healthy ones put back into the womb.

People with fertility problems may be desperate for a baby. But are all the treatments ethical?

Right or wrong?

Some people feel that fertility drugs shouldn't be used and IVF should never be carried out because they interfere with the natural processes of conception and birth. But banning these treatments would leave many people who desperately want to have babies very unhappy.

Other people believe that fertility treatment is acceptable in many circumstances, but object to its use in some particular cases—to enable a lesbian couple to have a child, for example.

Too old?

After a woman reaches the menopause, usually around her late 40s, she is no longer able to become pregnant naturally. Men, on the other hand, can become fathers into old age. Using IVF and a donor egg, doctors can enable an older woman to have a baby. This raises serious concerns about the physical fitness of the mother and how she may cope as she and her child grow older.

Should older women try to have babies? Should doctors help them to?

Ask yourself

◆ Do you think a woman of 62 should be able to have a baby if medical science can make it possible?
◆ How would you feel if your own mother was in her 70s now? How would it affect your life?

Case study

In 1994, Italian doctor Severino Antinori helped 62-year-old Rosanna della Corte have a baby through IVF. Many people objected to this, saying that the child would suffer from having such an old mother and that it was unnatural for her to conceive at her age. Della Corte wanted the child because she had recently lost her 17-year-old son in an accident.

New life

Extra embryos

IVF is expensive and it doesn't work every time. To reduce the cost and distress of extra treatment, it's usual to fertilize more eggs than necessary when starting an IVF program.

To increase the chances of success, two or three fertilized eggs are often put back into the woman's body. This means there's a high chance that IVF will lead to a multiple birth—having more than one baby. Usually, not all the eggs returned to the womb grow, but occasionally they do.

Fertility treatment often produces twins or triplets, but on occasions, has led to the birth of as many as six babies—sextuplets.

Case study

In 1996, Mandy Allwood took fertility medicine and became pregnant with eight babies (octuplets). She was warned early in the pregnancy that there was little chance all her babies would survive. To increase her chance of having any live babies, she was advised to have some of the embryos aborted. But she opted not to do this because she didn't want to choose to kill any of her babies. Eventually all eight unborn babies died. She was publicly criticized for her decision.

Unused embryos

Not all the fertilized eggs from an IVF programme are put into the woman's body. Extras are kept frozen so that they may be used later—if the first treatment doesn't work, or if the couple wants more children. Often these embryos are never required. Some "leftover" fertilised eggs are destroyed. Others may be used in medical research—we'll look at this in more detail later.

There can be difficult questions to answer when a couple doesn't use all the fertilized eggs that have been kept. There have been disputes in recent years when a couple has split up and one or other has wanted to destroy the fertilized eggs, or the woman has wanted to use a fertilized egg to create another baby but the man doesn't want her to.

"Spare" IVF embryos are frozen for future use. Who should decide what happens to them if they're not wanted later on, by one or both of the parents?

15

Avoiding illness

Some diseases are passed down through families in their genes (the chemical "instructions" that determine our individual characteristics). People with a genetic disease used to have a difficult choice to make. Should they avoid having children at all, or should they take a chance and hope their children would not inherit the disease?

With IVF, it's now possible to test fertilized eggs and only implant those that are healthy. Alternatively, a woman can become pregnant naturally, have the unborn baby tested, and then decide whether to end the pregnancy (have an abortion) if the baby is affected.

Even people who don't have a known genetic disorder often have their unborn babies screened for problems such as spina bifida and Down's syndrome. These are disorders that can be detected in the first half of a pregnancy and that have a serious impact on the child, if it is born. Many people who find they have an affected baby choose to abort it, but some keep the child, knowing what to expect.

Mending genes

As our knowledge about human genes increases, we will be able to screen unborn babies or fertilized eggs for more and more genetic disorders. It may even be possible to "mend" the genes in an unborn baby or fertilized egg some time in the fairly near future. There will be increasing pressure on people to have their babies screened and perhaps to continue only with completely healthy pregnancies.

Ask yourself

◆ Who should decide which disabilities make a life not worth living?
◆ Many disabled people live fulfilled lives —should they be denied the chance?

Ultrasound scans produce an image of the unborn baby that medical staff can use to check for multiple births as well as physical problems such as limb defects or missing internal organs.

Some people believe that life should be preserved at all costs and abortion should never be allowed. Other people think that every woman has a right to choose what happens to her body—and that may include choosing to end an unhealthy, or unwanted, pregnancy.

The abortion debate

Many people object to abortion and refuse to have their unborn children tested. They would continue with a pregnancy even if the child was bound to die. Other people think that it is wrong to bring a child into the world if it will have a short and painful life.

Religious background can have a strong bearing on opinion. Some religions, such as Catholicism, ban abortion completely. Orthodox Judaism allows it only to save the life of the mother. Some Buddhists think it is right if the child or mother would suffer greatly by continuing with the pregnancy, while others would not allow it at all.

In many countries, abortion is allowed until the fetus is about 24 weeks old. Modern intensive care units can often save babies born before this stage, though their good health can't always be guaranteed.

Ask yourself

◆ Do you think abortion is ever right?
◆ If a rape victim became pregnant, would abortion then be acceptable?
◆ What if a pregnant girl or woman was unfit to look after a child?
◆ Should every woman be able to choose whether or not to have an abortion, or should the law decide?
◆ If disability becomes rare because disabled babies are aborted, will our treatment of disabled people change?

Your life, your choice?

Usually, if we are ill we want to be cured. It's best if we can agree to and understand the treatments we are given. But sometimes we have to make decisions for people who can't make them for themselves—and occasionally people don't want treatment for one reason or another. These cases raise difficult ethical questions.

Saving babies

Even with modern screening techniques, not all babies are born healthy. Some are born long before the 40 weeks they need to grow fully in the womb have passed. These are called pre-term (premature) babies. Often they have not developed well enough to live outside the womb without advanced medical help.

Occasionally, parents may not want medical staff to try to save babies who will have a very difficult

With a lot of care and attention, many pre-term babies can be saved—but some will have serious disabilities or very poor health.

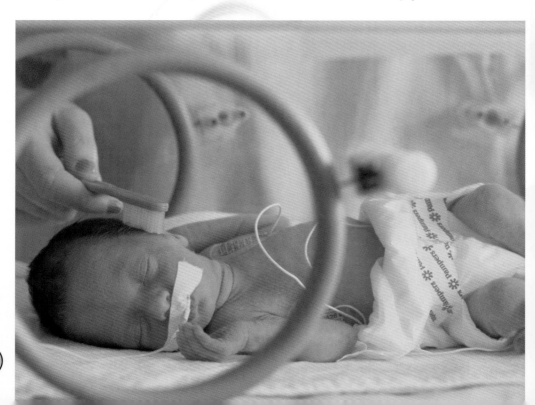

and painful life. Or they may have religious or moral objections to a treatment that's suggested, either for a baby or for an older child. Many Jehovah's Witnesses, for example, forbid some medical interventions. They would rather let themselves or their child die than accept a blood transfusion or an organ transplant. Sometimes, a court will decide to overrule the parents' authority and allow medics to carry out a treatment that the parents will not approve.

Conjoined twins are born when a fertilized egg begins to split into two separate embryos, but doesn't split completely. If the twins don't share vital organs, they can often be successfully separated, but in some cases only one can survive. The decision to lose one twin can be a heartbreaking one to make.

Case study

In 2001, conjoined twins called Rosie and Gracie Attard were born in England to a couple from Eastern Europe. They had traveled to England for the birth. The girls shared a heart, which was in Gracie's body cavity. The heart would not be strong enough to sustain both twins as they grew, so left together they would die within six months. Doctors decided that they would have to separate the twins by killing one of them—Rosie. The parents did not want doctors to operate as they refused to choose that one of their children should die. It was against their beliefs as Catholics. The English court ruled that the operation must be carried out and it was. Gracie survived.

Ask yourself

◆ Should we always do whatever we can to save a baby, regardless of the quality of life he or she can expect?
◆ Should courts or medical professionals be able to override parents' wishes?

Your life, your choice?

Giving consent

Parents need to make decisions about the medical care of their children, but usually we allow adults to make their own choices about the treatment they receive. In hospital, adults have to sign a consent form to say that they agree to a treatment. If they don't sign, the treatment usually can't be carried out. Consent isn't necessary in all cases. For example, if you were taken into hospital after a serious accident and you or your relatives were unable to give consent, emergency treatment would be carried out anyway.

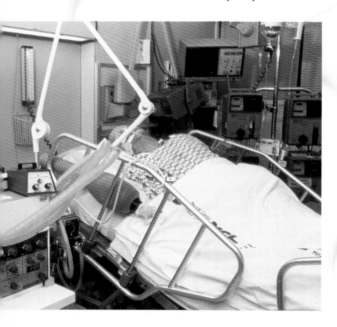

Some people make a "living will" in which they say whether they want to be kept alive artificially or if they'd rather be allowed to die.

Unable to choose

Some people are unable to give informed consent. Perhaps they are mentally disabled, or just don't understand the issues and so can't meaningfully agree to treatment. Or maybe they're unconscious and therefore unable to communicate. When someone is in this position, their closest relative may be asked to give consent for necessary treatment, but there are cases in which it's not clear whether treatment is necessary.

A particularly difficult example of this is people who have serious learning disabilities. They may not understand that if they have sex it could result in pregnancy. To become pregnant and have a baby (or an abortion) could be frightening and harmful for someone in this position. If a court declares a woman to be "incompetent", a guardian (someone appointed to look after her interests) can ask to have her sterilized.

Ask yourself

◆ Is it right to carry out surgery on someone who can't understand what is happening or why?
◆ Is it fair to sterilize a woman who is mentally unfit to have a baby, or is there another way to deal with the problem?
◆ What about men in a similar situation?

Refusing treatment

Sometimes people don't want the treatment that can save them. Their objection may be for religious or moral reasons—they might feel that transplanting organs from dead people is wrong, for example. Or, if they are very ill and in a lot of pain, they may feel that they have suffered enough and would rather die.

Occasionally, someone's decision to refuse treatment may seem to everyone else to be wrong. For example, a young woman with the eating disorder anorexia nervosa may not want treatment because she genuinely believes she is too fat. Her view of her body is distorted, and though she is likely to die of starvation, she may continue to refuse food and treatment. Her relatives will usually be keen for her to receive treatment and recover. People with other mental illnesses may also feel there is nothing wrong with them and refuse treatment.

Ask yourself

◆ Should we be able to override the wishes of someone whose illness itself leads them to refuse treatment?
◆ Who should choose whether an adult receives medical treatment?

An anorexia sufferer may refuse treatment and die. But it's the illness itself that causes her, or him, to reject help.

Your life, your choice?

Prevention and cure

Modern medicine has made great advances in preventing illness and disease. Health education encourages people to take regular exercise, eat a balanced diet, limit intake of alcohol, and avoid tobacco and other drugs. We are more aware than ever before of potential risks to our health.

Most people now know when they are making unhealthy lifestyle choices—are these choices ours to make?

Immunization programs have gone a long way towards wiping out some of the diseases that caused many deaths in the past. Most children in the world's richer countries are now vaccinated against diseases such as diptheria, measles, and tuberculosis. Large-scale programes in poorer countries have eliminated smallpox and nearly wiped out polio.

Vaccination concerns

Some people are worried about possible side effects of vaccination and would prefer not to have their children immunized against some diseases. In particular, the MMR vaccine (used in the U.K. since 1988) has been refused by many parents. This vaccine, used in 90 countries around the world, gives immunity to measles, mumps and rubella (German measles). Some people believe their children have developed autism (a condition affecting psychological development) after having the vaccine. Although this has not yet been clinically proven one way or the other, the claim has caused anxiety and has led other parents to refuse the vaccine.

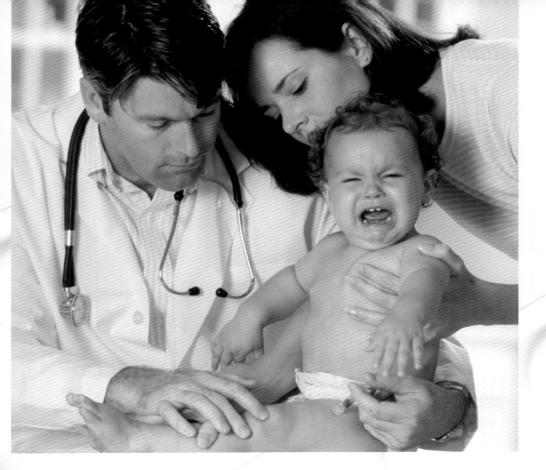

Risk of refusal

Mass immunization works only if most people have the vaccine. After MMR was introduced, epidemics of measles in the U.K. stopped occurring; deaths from measles fell from between 10 and 20 a year to zero. But if many people refuse the vaccine, the disease could re-emerge and some unvaccinated children will be damaged or die as a result.

Doctors are under pressure to persuade as many parents as possible to let their children have the MMR vaccine. In some cases, patients have been asked to find another doctor if they refuse the vaccine.

For a vaccine to wipe out a disease, it must be given to as many people as possible. Do people have a responsibility to accept vaccination?

Ask yourself

◆ Is it fair that some people should depend on the immunity of society as a whole to protect their children, refusing the vaccine themselves?

◆ Is it right for people to be removed from a doctor's list for refusing a vaccine, or should we all have the right to choose without it affecting the care offered to us in other ways?

A matter of life and death

We expect medical services to prolong life—but sometimes doctors need to choose a point at which to let someone die. How can this choice be made?

The right to die

Adults may refuse treatment if they are going to die and feel that treatment prolongs their suffering unnecessarily. Relatives may even make the decision to turn off a person's life-support system if doctors believe there is no chance of recovery. But, at the moment, the law in most countries doesn't allow euthanasia —helping people to die. Some people are concerned that if a person could choose to die, they may be put under pressure by their families to make the choice—or that people would be able to choose for others that they should be helped to die.

In 1999, Holland became the first country to make euthanasia legal. People there can ask their doctor to help them to die, and their doctor can legally help by giving them a drug that will speed-up their death.

Some people are afraid that we might use euthanasia as a way of getting rid of people no one wants to look after.

Do not resuscitate

If a person's heart stops beating, a specially-trained medical team can often resuscitate them—but they don't always do so. The doctors make a decision for each patient on whether it is worth resuscitating them. This will be based on any wishes the patient has expressed in advance, and the quality of life they can expect if they are resuscitated.

Demand for hospital beds is high. In 2000, U.K. hospitals were at the center of arguments about whether elderly patients were being allowed to die when they should have been resuscitated. Some people suggested that the National Health Service was trying to save money on caring for unwell elderly people by letting them die when they could be saved.

"No one... can arbitrarily choose whether to live or die; the absolute master of such a decision is the Creator alone."
POPE JOHN PAUL II, EVANGELIUM VITAE, MARCH 25 1995

"I am only 43 years old. I desperately want a doctor to help me to die."
DIANE PRETTY

Case study

In 2002, British woman Diane Pretty died of motor neurone disease at the age of 43. Before her death, she sought the right to have her husband help her to die so that she would not have to suffer a degrading deterioration and painful death. Her mental capabilities were unaffected by her disease. She asked for assurance that her husband would not be tried for murder if he helped her to die. Had she been physically able to kill herself, no one would have stopped her—but because the disease had wasted her muscles, she could not do it without help. Her requests were refused and she eventually died the slow and painful death she had been trying to avoid.

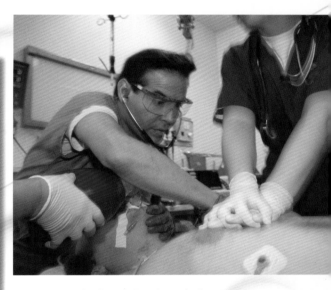

Who can judge whether it is "worth" resuscitating a very sick person whose quality of life on survival is likely to be poor?

Ask yourself

◆ Should Diane Pretty have been allowed help in dying as she wished?
◆ What would be the implications for other people who are similarly ill?
◆ How could we prevent people feeling pressurized to consent to assisted death?

A matter of life and death

Organ transplants

Since the 1960s, surgeons have been able to carry out transplants on some people whose organs aren't working properly. The process involves taking an organ—such as the heart, lungs, or liver—from someone who has died and using it to replace the defective organ. A patient who receives a transplant has to have treatment with medicines, too, so that their body doesn't reject the transplanted organ.

In most countries, patients or their relatives have to give permission for parts of their body to be used in transplant operations. Some people won't give permission as they fear that doctors will make less effort to keep them alive if they've said their organs can be used. Some people have religious or other objections to their body parts being used after death. But many people will gladly sign up as donors, in the knowledge that they could help to save someone's life.

Car-crash victims are common donors for transplant operations because they are often young people with healthy organs. How would you feel about parts of your body being used after your death?

Ask yourself

◆ Transplant organs are always required. Should we need permission to use organs, or should we insist that people say only if they *don't* want their organs to be used?
◆ Would it be acceptable for someone to receive an organ transplant but not want their own organs to be used for others?

Old and ill?

In the world's richer countries, people are living longer than ever before. Advances in healthcare mean that people recover from, or never get, some of the diseases that would have killed them a few decades ago. But as people become elderly, they are more likely to fall ill—and if they have an accident, they are more likely to suffer serious injury. This means that, as the population ages, the demands for healthcare increase.

In some countries the birthrate is falling, so the average age of the population is rising. Serious financial problems will occur if there are not enough young people to create the wealth needed to care for the older generation. In Japan, this is likely to become serious in the next 20 years.

Who will provide the wealth to care for an aging population? It's a problem we need to address.

Frozen for the future

Most of us accept that when we die, our physical life is over forever. But some wealthy people are paying large amounts of money for their dead bodies to be deep frozen. They hope that they will be revived at some point in the future when a cure for the condition that killed them has been found. This is called cryonics. There is no guarantee that it will work, or that anyone will want to revive them in the future.

Is being frozen for the future just a way of conquering fear of death? Are wealthy people being conned by cryonics?

Ask yourself

◆ Do you think it is bad for people to think they can come back after death?
◆ Would you want to be brought back to life long after your friends and family had all died?

Counting the cost

Healthcare is expensive. As we've seen, in some countries people have to pay for their own treatment, or take out insurance to cover the costs. In other countries, healthcare is free to anyone who needs it and is paid for by the government which collects money through taxes. In some poorer countries there is little available money for healthcare.

Public or private?

There can be advantages and disadvantages to both public (paid for from taxes) and private health-care systems. Some people say that where healthcare is free, people

Some complaints, such as varicose veins, are not life-threatening. Would as many people want treatment for these conditions if they had to pay?

demand more of it than they would if they had to pay. They may seek help for minor problems that they would perhaps ignore if they had to pay for treatment. They may expect quick, high-quality treatment, forgetting how many others are demanding the same. In reality, people often have to wait a long time for free treatment if their condition is not life-threatening.

Where private systems are in operation, treatments may be given sooner. But as people get older, or if they develop a medical condition that can't be completely cured, the cost of their health insurance increases— sometimes to the point where they can't afford it any more. If someone can't afford insurance or to pay for the treatments they need, they will face difficulties if they fall ill.

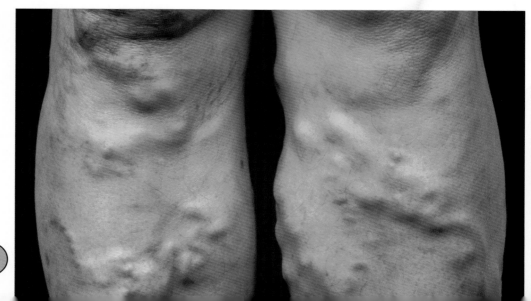

Spending the money

Most people accept that there is a limit to the amount of money any country can spend on healthcare. This means that there will always be choices to be made. In a country such as the U.K. where everyone contributes to the cost of healthcare, everyone has an interest in how the available money is spent. Some people object to spending it on treatments they don't consider especially important—fertility programs, for example. Others question whether we should buy very expensive medicines and treatments to prolong the life of people with illnesses that can't ultimately be cured.

"There will be... comprehensive medical treatment... for all citizens and their dependants which... will be without a charge on treatment at any point."
BEVERIDGE REPORT, 1942, WHICH LED TO THE SETTING UP OF THE UK'S NATIONAL HEALTH SERVICE

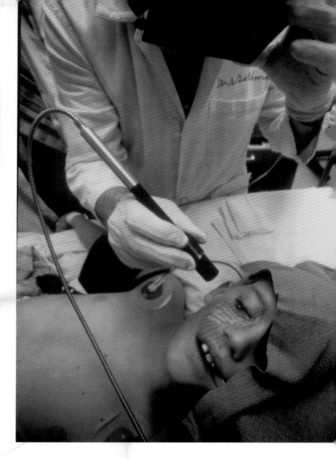

It's hard to judge what effects a severe scar or birthmark will have on someone's emotional health. Corrective treatments, such as laser surgery, are expensive. Should public money be spent on them, or on more "important" things?

Counting the cost

Profit and healthcare

Companies that develop new drugs and treatments usually do so to make money. Many of the treatments they produce cost so much that some countries just can't afford them. People in poorer countries often die from diseases that could easily be cured given funding. And even in a rich country like Britain, the NHS can't pay for some of the treatments that would help a lot of people. This means that some patients go without the best treatment, and may even die.

HOPITAL
FEDERATION INTERNATIONALE
DE LA CROIX-ROUGE ET DU
CROISSANT-ROUGE

Should we help provide poorer countries with decent healthcare at our own expense?

Ask yourself

◆ Should medical companies be able to charge so much for treatments that the people who need them can't afford them?
◆ Should there be a limit to the profit medical companies can make?

Who's responsible?

Some health problems can be traced to particular aspects of modern living. If someone suffers an accident at work, they can often claim compensation from their employer for their injury. Perhaps the employer should also pay for their treatment. Some problems can be traced to certain industries, too. The tobacco industry causes ill-health and costs countries a lot in medical care for smokers. And many people think that fumes from traffic fuel have caused an increase in childhood asthma.

Riding a motorcycle makes you more likely to have an accident than driving a car. People who choose to ride a motorbike are accepting a higher degree of risk. Who should pay for the risk—the makers of motorbikes? The riders?

fund asthma treatment, or extra tax on tobacco to pay for the treatment of smoking-related illnesses. Governments are careful to set taxation at just the right level to get as much money from the tax as they can. If the tax on, say, alcohol was too high, people may buy less of it and the government might collect less money in taxes overall.

Who should pay the medical costs of promoting unhealthy habits?

How much tax?

Adding a tax to some products to pay for the healthcare needs they create would make these items cost more. This might mean, for instance, paying more for gasoline and diesel to help

Ask yourself

◆ Would it be fair to tax industries that cause illness to pay for healthcare?
◆ Should we have to pay more for products that are bad for our health?

Testing, testing

Before a new treatment can be used, it has to be tested to make sure it's safe. Even then, mistakes are sometimes made and unsafe treatments harm people.

Why we test medicines

In the late 1950s and early 1960s, many pregnant women were given a drug called Thalidomide to cure morning sickness (being sick during pregnancy). But Thalidomide interfered with the development of the baby and some of the women gave birth to children with serious limb deformities. It took some time for people to realize and accept that Thalidomide was responsible, as doctors had not been careful to track what treatments they had given to women.

There have been other cases since of a medicine having an unwanted side effect—but none has been as serious as Thalidomide. Now all medicines must be tested thoroughly before they can be accepted for general use.

How we test medicines

There are several stages in the testing of modern medicines. First, they may be tested on simple living cells in a laboratory to make sure they do what they're supposed to do. Then they may be tested on animals—not only in normal doses, but also in very large doses given over a long period of time. Finally, clinical trials are carried out on real patients.

Animal testing

Specially bred animals—often mice, dogs, and monkeys—are used at different stages of the testing process for new medicines and other treatments. Medical researchers involved in animal testing claim that it's often the only way they can test new treatments thoroughly. If they had tested Thalidomide on pregnant mice, for example, perhaps the problems would have been detected. They say that they are justified in using animals if the results of their work will save human lives, or relieve human suffering.

Thalidomide caused 10,000 people to be born with disabilities— usually limb deformities.

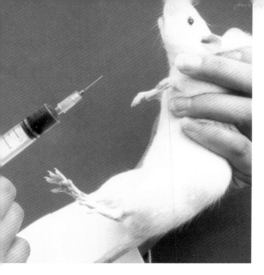

Is it fair to breed animals especially for testing—knowing that they will suffer—even if it is for our benefit?

People who are against animal testing say that much of the work could be carried out on tissue cultures —samples of body tissue grown in a lab—instead of making animals suffer. Many say that we don't have the right to make animals suffer, and some religions forbid killing animals or causing them pain or stress. Already, testing of cosmetics on animals has been greatly reduced because of public opinion. If enough people objected to testing medical treatments on animals, maybe this would also stop in time.

"Aware of the suffering caused by the destruction of life, I vow to cultivate compassion and learn ways to protect the lives of people, animals, plants, and minerals."

FIRST BUDDHIST PRECEPT,
THICH NHAT HANH

Case study

Animals may be used in the development of medical technology as well as for testing treatments. Scientists have implanted electrodes into the brains of monkeys to intercept electrical signals sent by the brain when the monkey moves its limbs. By working with these signals, they have been able to get a robotic arm to move in the same way as the monkey's own arm. Researchers hope to use this technology to enable people to move artificial limbs through thought—just as they'd move their real limbs.

Ask yourself

◆ Is animal life less important than human life?

◆ Do we have the right to test medical treatments on some animals but not on others? If so, on what grounds?

◆ If you knew someone who had a serious disease like cancer, would you accept animal testing if it helped in the development of a cure?

◆ If a new medicine had never been tested on a living thing, but only on cells in a lab, would you be happy about being the first person to try it?

Testing, testing

Clinical trials

People must give consent before new treatments can be tested on them, and a committee of experts must examine and approve the proposal.

Usually, a group of patients is given a new treatment and a similar group is given an identical-looking placebo—a "medicine" that has no effect. In this way, no one can tell whether or not they are getting the real medicine. The doctors or nurses who give people the treatment or placebo don't know which is which either, so that their own knowledge can't affect the results of the test.

After a period of treatment, all the patients are tested in the same ways. From the results, the researchers can find out if the medicine works, and if it has any unwanted side effects.

A placebo looks the same as a real drug. If testers don't know whether or not the medicine they are taking is real, they're less likely to report effects that aren't genuine.

Ask yourself

◆ Is it right to give placebos to people who are hoping for treatment?
◆ Imagine you took part in a medical trial where the tested drug was successful. How would you feel if you found out later that you'd been given a placebo and that your illness had now progressed too far to be cured?

Choosing risk

The process of testing medicines takes a very long time, often many years. While a drug is being tested, it can't be prescribed as it hasn't been approved for general use. Yet someone who has a terminal illness may be willing to try any treatment, even if it's not certain that it will work and even if it could produce horrible side effects. Approval of tested drugs could come too late for some patients. Is this fair?

A lot of early medical research involved studying dead bodies that had been stolen from gallows or graves. Does it matter how we gain our medical knowledge?

Case study

In December 2002 the British High Court ruled that a treatment for the deadly brain disease CJD could be tried on two dying teenagers, even though it hadn't been tested thoroughly. The teenagers had no chance of recovery—even if the new treatment turned out to be effective—but their parents asked doctors to try it in the hope of prolonging their children's lives and helping to find a cure for other CJD sufferers.

Medical ethics

These days, hospitals and researchers are watched closely to make sure that people are treated fairly and ethically during medical trials. In the past, this hasn't always been the case. During the 1950s, for example, the U.S. army tested soldiers with large doses of radiation, in order to find out if it had any harmful effects. Many of the soldiers later fell ill or died as a result. The knowledge we've gained from this has been valuable. But can we ever feel comfortable using it?

Ask yourself

◆ How should we treat knowledge that has been gained in an unethical way? Does it give some value to the victims' suffering if we use what we've learned to help others? Or does this show lack of respect?

Tomorrow's treatments

Scientists are finding more and more sources for new medical treatments. If you were very ill, you may not care where the treatment used to cure you came from. But as a society, we set some limits. How do we balance what we consider right, or fair, with our desire to cure as many people as possible?

It doesn't look like a baby yet, but given the chance to grow this group of stem cells could become a person.

Stem cells

Stem cells are the first cells produced when a fertilized human egg begins to divide. They are the cells that would, if the egg were left to grow in a woman's body, develop into a whole human baby. At the earliest stage, all the cells are exactly the same. But each has the information and the potential to grow into any kind of cell in the human body. It is from stem cells that our internal organs—skin, blood, and bone—all grow.

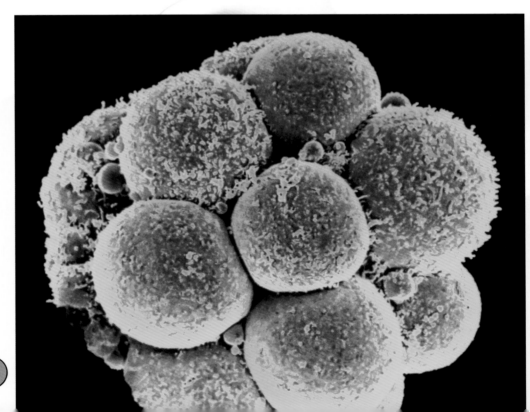

Stem cell research

The growth potential of stem cells makes them extremely valuable for medical research. Scientists believe that in the future we should be able to work from stem cells to create, for example, real skin to use in skin grafts, and treatments for conditions such as diabetes.

Clone your own

Our bodies are designed to reject foreign tissue. This means that people who receive organ transplants have to be given medicines to prevent their bodies rejecting the new material. One day, we might be able to grow tissue that is exactly like that in our own bodies. We could do this by creating clones from our own tissues and using the stem cells from these. A clone has exactly the same genetic make-up as its "parent," so anything grown from its stem cells would be accepted by the parent's body.

Ethical problems

At the moment, stem cells can only be used from fertilized eggs left over from IVF programmes. Some people believe that a fertilized egg counts as a human baby. Whether or not a fertilized egg should be considered a human life depends on when you think life begins. The Catholic church teaches that life begins as soon as the egg is fertilized. Traditional Jewish belief is that life begins when the

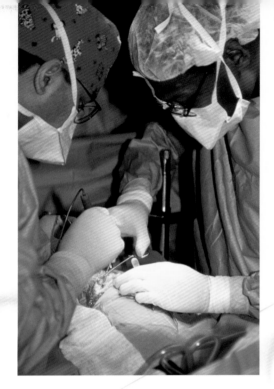

Transplants are very complex operations and a patient runs the risk of rejecting the donated organ. Could cloning offer a solution to this problem?

baby's head has emerged at birth. Other people place the start of life at different points between these stages, but typically at around 90 days after fertilization.

Ask yourself

◆ Is it right to use "spare" fertilized eggs either for research or to make body tissues for use in medical treatments?
◆ Would your answer be different if there was no intention to create a baby in the first place—if we "grew" stem cells just for medical purposes?

Tomorrow's treatments

Transplant options

Each year, 20 times as many organs are needed for transplant as actually become available—so often people die while waiting for a donor. As there aren't enough organs, scientists have tried to find new ways of getting the body parts needed.

One area now being researched is the use of animal organs. Pigs' bodies are similar in many ways to human bodies, and eventually we may be able to use organs from pigs to transplant into people. However, the rejection problems that occur with transplanted human organs will be much worse with organs coming from different animals.

Could we soon be farming pigs for hearts, just as we farm them for bacon?

Engineering organs

Genetic engineering involves changing the genes of a plant or animal to alter some of its characteristics. Scientists have created genetically-engineered pigs whose hearts won't be rejected by the human body. It's likely that in a few years, pigs will be farmed to provide organs for transplant. A transplant from a different animal is called a xenographic transplant.

Ask yourself

◆ Is it right to create and kill animals specifically for transplants?
◆ Is it any different from breeding and killing animals to eat?
◆ How would you feel about having a pig's heart?

By changing the genetic code of the chicken, we could soon get human chemicals from eggs.

Medicine farms

It's not just transplant organs that can be "grown" through other animals. We already use different species to create some medicines.

People with diabetes are unable to produce a chemical called insulin. Without injections of insulin, they become ill and may die. Insulin used to be taken from pigs and cows. It was treated chemically before being given to people. Now, human insulin can be produced using genetically-modified bacteria. The bacteria—tiny micro-organisms—are grown in large vats and produce insulin which is taken away and turned into the medicine that diabetics need.

Scientists are working on making genetic changes to some animals so that they will produce insulin and other human chemicals that some patients need. They're looking at whether it would be possible to get goats or sheep to produce such chemicals in their milk, or chickens to produce them in their eggs. It might be easy and cheap to create them in these ways.

Another possibility is using animals to create milk that's identical to human breast milk. Women who can't or don't want to breastfeed their babies have to use formula milk, which is made from cows' milk with specially added chemicals. But this is not exactly the same as human milk. A genetically-modified cow, sheep, or goat could possibly produce milk that is the same as human milk. This would give women who don't breastfeed their babies an alternative that's as nutritious as the real thing.

Ask yourself

◆ Is it acceptable to change other species so that they can produce something we want or that may save human lives?
◆ Perhaps you feel it depends on the species—that maybe it's all right to change a bacterium, but not a cow or pig? Where would you draw the line?

One for all?

W'e're not all the same and we don't all want the same things. Yet some of our healthcare choices are made by governments or other bodies who act for everyone at once. How much right do we have to make individual choices?

Public health

Most countries have departments of public health. These are government departments with responsibility for trying to keep the people in the country as healthy as possible. They take actions that will affect everyone.

Issues that seem totally unrelated to medicine can still affect our health. By causing pollution, traffic becomes a health problem as well as a transport issue.

Case study

In the mid-20th century, governments in many richer countries followed advice from scientists and added a chemical called fluoride to drinking water. The reason for doing this was to reduce tooth decay, particularly in children. There was no way to avoid having the fluoride apart from never drinking mains water. Since then, it's been found that too much fluoride can can cause teeth to develop brown spots, and even dents or pits. But a whole generation of children and adults have had fluoride added to their water. In the U.S., water still contains fluoride in many areas.

Ask yourself

◆ Is it right to add extra chemicals to food or drink that we can't avoid, in the hope of keeping most people healthy?
◆ Is it a good thing, aiming to improve the health of many people—or a bad thing, denying us choice and maybe harming a few people?

A personal issue

Most of us feel that our health is a personal matter. We generally want details of our bodies to be private, and, as individuals, we want choices in the way our healthcare is handled.

But governments have to plan public healthcare for the future, and to do this they need details about us. They also want to streamline the treatments on offer to make the medical system as efficient, quick, and cheap as possible. Sometimes a compromise is needed, but it isn't always something we are happy with.

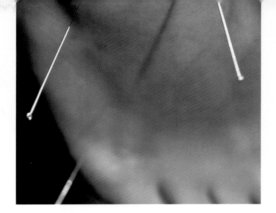

Should we be told about all the treatments available when we're ill? Would this include alternative treatments such as acupuncture?

Supermarkets store information about what people buy. In 2000, the U.K. government wanted access to these details in order to find links between diet and health, but the supermarkets would not allow it.

Choosing treatments

If you go to a doctor for help with a common problem, he or she will probably offer you a fairly standard treatment. It will have been used effectively on many other people. Unless you have special medical knowledge, you're unlikely to know of any other options. Sometimes there are better treatments, but they cost more and so aren't offered to people. If you have an interest in alternative therapies, you might want to try a different type of treatment—such as homeopathy or acupuncture. But, perhaps because many doctors are suspicious of techniques that haven't been tested as thoroughly as standard medicines, you may not be told about them. Even if you were told, you'd probably have to pay privately for this different kind of treatment.

Ask yourself

◆ Might it be too difficult, complicated, or upsetting for some people to have to think about their treatment options—isn't that what we pay doctors for?
◆ How can we make sure that people understand all the information they are being given?

One for all?

Online medicine

More and more people have access to the Internet, either at home, at work, or in a public setting such as a school, library, or cybercafé. There is a lot of medical information available on the Internet and many people use it to find out more about medical problems. Some even try to work out for themselves what is wrong with them if they feel unwell.

The Internet can be a valuable source of self-help and a useful way to communicate with other sufferers. People with a rare condition, who may not have a fellow sufferer to talk to locally, may be able to find someone using the Internet.

Some doctors find it threatening or difficult to deal with patients who have researched their illnesses online. The doctors may not be able to offer some of the treatments the patients have read about. Or the patient may have used an unreliable source—or misunderstood the information they found—and perhaps wrongly identified their illness.

Laws and lifestyle

Our lifestyles affect our health in many ways. Most governments use education and laws to try to protect the health of the people in their

Does medical information on the Internet empower patients or make doctors' lives more difficult?

countries. For example, a law that says you must wear a seat belt in a car is intended to cut the number of deaths and injuries in road accidents. We have laws that forbid the use of many drugs because they are harmful to our health. And we have laws that say food in restaurants must be prepared in hygienic conditions to protect us from food poisoning.

But governments can't protect our health entirely. We also have to make intelligent choices and act wisely. Although it is illegal not to wear a seat belt, there's no one checking we wear one whenever we're in a car.

Should we limit the law?

Some people think that the government interferes too much with our lives and we should be given more choice in how we live. Others think that there should be many laws to protect us and our health—especially in countries where everyone shares the cost of everyone else's medical treatment.

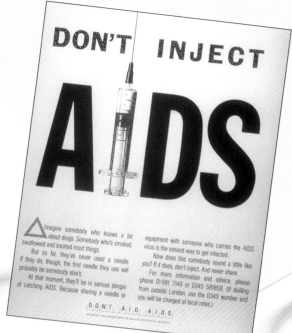

DON'T INJECT AIDS

Imagine somebody who knows a bit about drugs. Somebody who's smoked, swallowed and snorted most things.

But so far, they've never used a needle. If they do, though, the first needle they use will probably be somebody else's.

At that moment, they'll be in serious danger of catching AIDS. Because sharing a needle or equipment with someone who carries the AIDS virus is the easiest way to get infected.

Now does this somebody sound a little like you? If it does, don't inject. And never share.

For more information and advice, please phone 01-981 7140 or 0345 581858. (If dialling from outside London, use the 0345 number and you will be charged at local rates.)

DON'T AID AIDS

ISSUED BY THE DEPARTMENT OR HEALTH AND SOCIAL SECURITY

Governments use publicity campaigns to try to encourage us to be healthy—but we're used to advertising telling us to do something, not to avoid something, so the campaigns may not work.

Case study

In 2002, a group of Americans brought a legal case against the McDonald's burger chain, claiming it sold unhealthy foods that made them obese. Do you think McDonald's was to blame? Can we expect people to know that eating a lot of this kind of food will be bad for them, or should companies like McDonald's issue health warnings?

Ask yourself

◆ Do you think governments should pass lots of laws to try to preserve our health, or should we be responsible?
◆ If you live in a country in which healthcare is mostly free, do you think every person has a duty to live a healthy life in order to reduce the need for expensive treatment?

Who cares?

We've seen throughout this book how our health is governed by many different aspects of our lives—such as our living conditions, food and the environment. But who is monitoring the care we receive from health services, or the risks posed to us by other industries or situations that affect our well-being? And how much responsibility do we have for the well-being of other people around the world?

Ethics committees

In many countries, developments in medicine, research, and the behavior of medical professionals are carefully watched by ethics committees. These are groups of people who meet to discuss the work carried out in research institutions and hospitals. They include medical professionals and philosophers interested in ethics.

An ethics committee tries to represent the views of everyone who will have an interest in an issue and make decisions about what is right and wrong. An ethics committee in a hospital might discuss the case of an individual patient. Or a similar group might be appointed by the government to discuss whether research into a particular area should be allowed.

The rights and wrongs of testing treatments on animals might be discussed by an ethics committee.

Legal protection

Regulations about who may practice medicine are intended to protect us from people who are underqualified or even intend harm. These rules change over time, to keep up with the needs of society. In the U.K., for example, the pressure on doctors in hospitals is increasing. So moves are being made to allow some nursing staff to carry out various procedures that previously only doctors could do. By law, the nurses will be trained and tested to required standards.

National laws to protect health do not just affect medical services. They apply to many other aspects of life, too—how long we're allowed to work without a break for food or rest, which pesticides farmers may use, how food should be packaged and stored in shops, and so on.

International laws

Although most laws are specific to individual countries, there is global agreement about some matters. The World Health Organization and the World Medical Association are two international bodies who work to protect health around the world. The World Health Organization works in areas of medicine, and also to relieve famine and poverty. Its aim is to eradicate disease and offer all people "a state of complete physical, mental and social well-being.".

The World Medical Association has declared that all doctors must make the following promises:

"I will practice my profession with conscience and dignity; the health of my patient will be my first consideration; I will respect the secrets which are confided in me, even after the patient has died… I will not permit consideration of religion, nationality, race, party, politics, or social standing to intervene between my duty and my patient; I will maintain the utmost respect for human life from its beginning, even under threat, and I will not use my medical knowledge contrary to the laws of humanity…"

Can we ever attain a state where good healthcare will be available to everyone, wherever they are in the world?

Your own opinion

By now you should have enough background knowledge to start to form your own views on modern medicine. These may be the same as or different from your friends'. But keep asking questions and finding things out. Try to understand all sides of the story. The more you learn, the stronger your arguments will be.

Further work

Here are some ideas to help you investigate health issues and learn more about modern medicine.

Your health, your choice?

Find out what your school does to protect your health. For example, are you encouraged to join after-school sports clubs, or to cycle to school? How (if at all) does the school help you to eat healthily at lunchtime? Do they make healthy meals cheaper than unhealthy ones? Does the school sell unhealthy snacks?

Who else takes responsibility for keeping you healthy? Does anyone make you do some physical exercise each week? Are you encouraged to eat a healthy diet and drink plenty of water at home? How could you improve your own lifestyle to help you stay healthy?

Health rules

Find out how school rules and the law work to protect your health. For example, do you have compulsory sports classes? Are there restrictions on what you can or can't handle or do in science lessons? Is there anything you're not allowed to bring in for lunch? What other health and safety regulations do you come across every day?

Your medication

If you take any regular medication, find out all you can about how it's produced, how it's been tested, and how researchers are trying to improve the treatments available. Are you happy with the way the treatments have been developed and tested? Would treatment be available to you if you lived in a poorer country?

Useful websites

www.healthfinder.gov
Reliable health information on U.S. healthcare—health insurance, Medicare, Medicaid etc—as well as a "kids" area with games and contests.
www.medicare.gov
Explains U.S. government healthcare for people aged over 65, and some younger people with disabilities.
www.medicaidmadeeasy.com
Explains the U.S. program to help those on low incomes.

Make a difference

◆ Unless you have objections to organ transplants, find out how to register as an organ donor in your country.
◆ Take an interest in the products you buy. Find out how and where they were produced and decide whether you should continue buying them.

Glossary

AIDS (Acquired Immune Deficiency Syndrome) A disease in which the body's ability to fight disease is destroyed and the person slowly dies from catching other infections.

anorexia nervosa An eating disorder in which sufferers lose dangerous amounts of weight because they have a distorted body image and believe they are too fat.

autism A medical condition in which sufferers have difficulty relating to and communicating with others.

blood clot A lump of congealed blood that forms in the bloodstream. It may travel to a vital organ, such as the lungs or brain, and cause injury or death.

BSE (Bovine Spongiform Encephalopathy) A disease that attacks the brains of cattle, leading eventually to death. The human form of the disease is called CJD (Creutzfeldt-Jacob Disease).

clone An exact genetic copy of a single plant or animal.

Down's syndrome A genetic disorder in which sufferers usually have learning difficulties and recognizable physical characteristsics, but no physical deformity.

embryo The early stage of a developing baby. In humans, a baby is called an embryo from the second to the eighth week of pregnancy.

epidemic A widespread occurrence of a disease.

fetus A developing baby after its main body parts have formed. In humans, a baby is called a fetus from the ninth week of pregnancy until birth.

genes The means by which we inherit features from our parents and ancestors.

genetic disease An illness caused by a problem with genes. Genetic diseases are passed on through families.

lesbian A woman who prefers to have another woman as her sexual partner rather than a man.

malaria A blood disease caused by a parasite and spread by mosquitoes. It kills 2.7 million people a year, mostly in tropical areas.

menopause Physical changes in a woman's body that usually begin in her late 40s. They mark the end of the period when she can naturally bear children.

spina bifida A condition that causes a gap in the spine, between vertebrae, leading to problems with the nervous system and often paralysis.

sterilize To make someone incapable of producing any children.

vaccination ("immunization") Giving someone a weakened form of a disease—usually by injection—to encourage the body to defend itself against the full form of the disease.

Index